Lipstick, Red! I Am Me!

*The Attributes That Exemplify the
Essence of a Woman*

For my daughters, Mom, Dad, Papa, Sisters, Brothers, Grandparents, Aunts, Uncles, Relatives, Ancestors, Teachers, Friends, Central Magnet High School Class of 1999, Wesleyan College (First for Women), and To All "Lipstick Red" Women and Girls All Over The World...Thank You!

Lipstick, Red! I Am Me!

The Attributes That Exemplify the
Essence of a Woman

A. Williams

VMH Publishing
Atlanta, GA

VMH Publishing
3355 Lenox Rd.NE Ste 750 Atlanta, GA 30326
www.vmhpublishing.com

Copyright © 2019 by Arletha Williams

All rights reserved.

This book may not be reproduced in whole or in part, in any form or by means, electronic or mechanical, including photocopying, recording, or by any information storage and retrieval system now known or hereafter invented, without permission from the publisher.

Bulk Ordering Information:

Quantity sales. Special discounts are available on quantity purchases by corporations, associations, and others. For details, contact the publisher at the address above or via email at: info@vmhpublishing.com

Book Cover Design: VMH Publishing
Cover Image: Shutterstock
Interior Layout: VMH Publishing
Editor: Sara Prescott

Hardback ISBN: 978-1-9479284-9-7

Made in United States of America

10 9 8 7 6 5 4 3 2 1

This book is presented to:

_____

_____

By:

_____

_____

On this date:

_____

_____

"I am 'Lipstick, Red!' I am me! I am unique and this is my decree."
- Arletha

Contents

Preface	I
Introduction	II
1. Get Out of Your Box!	15
2. So…What Exactly is "Lipstick Red?"	23
3. "Lipstick, Red" is Bold	29
4. "Lipstick, Red" is Beautiful	45
5. "Lipstick, Red" is Daring	51
6. "Lipstick, Red" is Confident	57
7. "Lipstick, Red" is Graceful	63
8. "Lipstick, Red" is Timeless	69
9. "Lipstick, Red" is Unmatched	77
10. "Lipstick, Red" Does Not Envy	83
11. The Essence of "The Woman"	89
"Lipstick Red" Inspiration, "You Are Enough" Poem	97
"Lipstick Red" Poem	99
My Lipstick Red Journey (20 Questions & Reflections)	103

Preface

I decided to write this book because there are so many women in society who wish to be like other women. We want to be like them, both in outward appearance and inward characteristics; we want what they have, and to be able to do what they do. Women find themselves wishing to be completely different people, and ignoring their own uniqueness and what they have going for themselves. Do you know this affects your self-esteem?

What happened to living life as you were destined to live, and not getting so easily distracted by what others say and deem acceptable? What happened to all women just loving themselves for who they are and not trying to conform to a certain ideal or standard? What happened to realizing that each individual woman has something interesting to bring to the table? Has this spirit of individuality and self-worth disappeared? Well, I am here to remind you that you are "Lipstick Red"... a term I coined to represent a confident, beautiful, and intelligent woman. One who knows her value. There is no one in the world we can be but to be ourselves, and there's power in that. We were not created by God to be 'her,' but to be ourselves. Consequently, that means we have a purpose only we can fulfill and there is a need in the world only we can remedy. We as women must embrace the power and abilities that only we possess. No one can be you and no one can be me.

That is why this book challenges the status quo. It not only explains how to recognize our value and worth, but it also reminds us that we are allowed to just be ourselves. When we are not trying to be like others or conforming to societal expectations, that means we are no longer in competition. This allows us to make that first step toward accepting ourselves. No one needs to give you permission to do this critical thing. When you embrace yourself just as you are, it can radically transform your life.

This book calls on you to tap into those qualities, talents, and attributes that make you who you are. It challenges you to be "Lipstick Red," and be confident in yourself. Perhaps, most importantly, it challenges you to be *you*. Your own self-expression of your gifts will act as a witness to other people around you. What you eventually choose to say or do will have an impact on women of all ages. Go ahead, be "Lipstick Red." You'll find that you always had it inside of you.

Introduction

Hey, "Lipstick Red" Woman! What is it about you that sets you apart from everyone else? Don't let anyone fool you — you are a beautiful work of art, complete with colorful lines and dots, jagged edges, and soft curves. All put together to create a masterpiece that is uniquely and wonderfully you.

How do you define yourself? Are you outgoing? Introverted? Confident? Are you living a fulfilled life as a woman? Do you embody what it means to be 'Lipstick Red'?

Red lipstick itself is a work of art. In comparison to other shades, wearing the color red exudes confidence, boldness, and sophistication. Likewise, women who show themselves love and know their worth begin to exhibit those qualities as well. Once we come into our own fullness, we may begin to live more satisfied lives. It starts with you embracing your own version of "Lipstick, Red." It helps to build your self-worth and your self-esteem. Besides, if you don't do it, who else will do it for you? It doesn't take much. Just give it a try!

The following is a proclamation that you should learn and recite to yourself each day. It will give you a boost in times when you need assurance:

"I am "Lipstick, Red!" I am bold. I am beautiful. I am daring. I am confident. I am graceful. I am timeless. I am unmatched. I am uniquely me! From the hair on top of my head, to the brain I have inside...from the fullness of my breasts, no matter what size, to my hips that give me my core, and from my gorgeous legs...I am "Lipstick, Red!" I am me. I am unique and this is my decree."

Chapter 1 - Get Out of Your Box!

"Women are the largest untapped reservoir of talent in the world." - Hillary Clinton

As women, it can be challenging to express ourselves or invest in our unique attributes because we spend so much time feeding into and idolizing other people's. More often than not, we lose precious time to nurture ourselves and explore our own "self." We must realize that we as individuals are also important and need the same encouragement and enhancement we give to others, if not more. Usually we just don't pour that same sparkle and shine on ourselves and into our own lives. Interestingly enough, by the time we turn around, our energy simply amounts to table scraps that no one can use. Not even our own "Self." We must reassess making ourselves a priority and strive to come into the fullness of our own art and grace as individual women. Yes, this requires deep introspection and self-reflection, and it challenges you to ask yourself, "Who am I?" But considering these things will ultimately help you in establishing your own confidence.

What are you waiting for [insert name here]? I implore you to get out of your box! You can't hide your gift from the world. Do you even know you were born with a special gift? Our special gifts are revealed when we come into our full potential. You will not know who you are if you are constantly striving to be someone else. You will not know who you are if you do not discover yourself. Oftentimes, nothing is happening inside that box but darkness, loneliness, and confinement. This is because you don't realize exactly who you are inside.

Living life in your comfort zone is your way of accepting things as they are and remaining stagnant. In order to get where we want to be in life, we must be willing to place ourselves in uncomfortable situations in order to conquer these areas and grow. It takes hard work and sacrifice. You can't let fear or idleness stop you, "Lipstick Red" woman! Get out of that box! Don't conceal your gift. It is meant for you to use to enhance the world in some way, so you must give birth to it. You must shed some light on it. Some little girl in this world is waiting for your example so they can witness the confidence and certainty of a real woman. Where are you? You cannot find your true essence as a woman if you are stuck in a box. Snap out of it! You can't hide your wonderful gift any longer! There are six sides to that box that are limiting the potential that was intended for you. That box is placing a thick barrier around your destiny!

Quite like in the "Allegory of the Cave" by the ancient Greek orator and rhetor Plato, until you begin to see the light, you can't move toward your own liberation. You cannot be free. You cannot embrace "Lipstick Red." When you make the decision to be a "Lipstick Red" woman, you are making a conscious effort to value yourself and your needs, as well as not letting people's perception of you dictate your actions. Your "self" is waiting to express itself through you. Wake her up and get her going!

You see, when you get outside of your comfort zone, you see the world differently. You no longer place limits on yourself, as you have stepped outside those limits. You see a world where you can dream bigger dreams and realize a more confident you. You have the freedom and will to envision yourself in the way you were meant to be. [Insert your name here], you do not need permission to make a positive impact on humanity. You see, when you get out of your box, you step into a place where dreams come alive and you have the freedom and will to envision yourself in the way you were meant to be. It is a wonderful thing to experience, because you are not confined, constrained, nor contained by anything or anyone. When you step *outside* the box, you step *into* freedom. There are no boundaries for accepting who you are in your life. Live it! Dream it! Believe in it!

Chapter 1: Reader's Notes

Chapter 2 - So... What Exactly is "Lipstick, Red?"

"Lipstick Red" exemplifies that there is no substitute for the essence of your womanness!" - A. Williams

Yes, [insert your name here], "Lipstick Red" is the phrase of the hour! The term is meant to signify positive attributes of a unique and confident woman. Being "Lipstick Red" is again not letting circumstances define you, and tackling life with that 'girl boss' attitude so that you can fulfill your goals and live your best life. There are seven main aspects of being "Lipstick Red" that are inherently a part of you; all you must do is believe them and channel them. They are as follows: boldness, inner beauty, daring, confidence, gracefulness, timelessness, and being unmatched. Yes, [insert your name here],you need all seven in order to more clearly and profoundly express the essence of your "womanness." There are hundreds more positive and helpful attributes that aid in your growth as a woman, but these main characteristics help set the tone.

The goal of this book is to equip you with key values that are not only to be implemented and cherished by you, but also taught to other women in our world. Once you adopt them, you should find yourself transformed...inside and out. You will carry yourself in a different way that exudes both boldness and assuredness.

You must believe in these qualities about yourself; adopt them, learn them, practice them, be them, recognize them in other women, and teach them after you have sown them into yourself. These attributes will reap a bountiful harvest for you as you seek to come to, as Oprah Winfrey says, your best "self." They will give you the freedom, expression, and responsibility to come into your own person. "Lipstick Red" is you! It is your womanness. It is your essence. It is you in your pureness and your individuality.

Cheers to the smile you get in the mirror when you see a reflection of yourself! Cheers to expressing your "womanness!" Cheers to being equipped with the tool that exudes your class, your confidence, your uniqueness, your strength, and so much more! Cheers to the refreshing breath of coming into the fullness of your "Self!"

In the next chapters, we will discuss each of the attributes mentioned in more detail so that you can easily work on these areas in your life.

Chapter 2: Reader's Notes

Chapter 3 - "Lipstick, Red" is Bold

"A woman is like a tea bag; you never know how strong it is until it is in hot water."- Eleanor Roosevelt

To be bold is a must. What decision are you holding back from, [insert your name here]? What choices do you need to make in order to express the boldness you possess and move forward, [insert your name here]? Go for it! Do those things! Since "Lipstick Red" is bold, we must be courageous and unafraid in pursuit of whatever it is we need to do. Don't hold back. Discover the boldness that lies within you.

At times, some women are reluctant to make a bold fashion statement. This may stem from fear of going against societal standards traditionally set in place for how a woman 'should' look. It may also stem from fear of judgment, or even negative, unwanted attention.

You may question if you're being too loud or flashy with your choice of dress. Well, I am here to tell you...who cares? Why *not* be unapologetic in your fashion choices? Your style is an outward expression of who you are and your personality. Now, I am not saying to disregard class, however, as there is always a time and place for everything. I am saying, though, to try something different. This could be the nudge you need to try that little something you have always wanted to, but never actually had the courage to put your foot down and do it. This applies to fashion or otherwise. Is this something you can relate to [insert your name here]? If it is, go ahead! Try that pencil skirt with stilettos! Dress up your work outfit with statement earrings! Wear a bright lipstick with a plain white t-shirt! Try whatever it is that will make you happy; it will certainly challenge your confidence and take you out of your comfort zone.

Another example of being bold is being more experimental with your cooking. What's holding you back, [insert your name here]? Get in that kitchen and cook. Try new recipes beyond your basic spaghetti. You will not only enjoy more variety in your food, but you will expand your arsenal of skills!

Boldness can also look like asking for what you want. Is it that promotion you know you deserve at work, but no one has approached you? Well, [insert your name here], ask! You can do it. How can people give us what we want if they do not know about it? Matthew 7:7-8 says, "Ask, and it shall be given you; seek, and ye shall find; knock, and it shall be opened unto you:

For every one that asketh receiveth; and he that seeketh findeth; and to him that knocketh it shall be opened." This concept can be applied to anything we desire in life.

One of my best expressions of boldness was when I decided to leave an unhealthy and unfruitful marriage. I was mentally, physically, and verbally abused by a person whom I trusted and would have liked to have been with for life. Well, things just did not work out. You see, sometimes, we do not really know our mate until it is too late. A partner can act one way at first, but farther along into a relationship or marriage their true colors can start to show.

When the cycle of abuse begins, it is really hard to interrupt. There is a kind of familiarity and security in the constant routine of destructive behavior. There is a sense of hope because you believe the person in question can change. More often than not, this is not the case. People do not typically change for other people; they change for themselves. The decision to walk away when I finally did was not easy, but when I realized that my partner and I were not equally yoked, something had to change. When I realized my self-worth and that having constant anxiety was not good for me, I had to get out of that box. The marriage box, in my opinion, should be different from all others. It should be one whereas both husband and wife can express themselves uniquely, while still being mindful of each other's needs and desires, within reason. Both people should treat each other with kindness and respect, without it resulting in mental or physical harm.

In my marriage, my partner did not want me to visit my family, or even his family for that matter. He prayed for evil things to happen to me, like hoping my car would break down when I tried to attend a graduation for one of his older daughters (and it did). He would call me names like "nigger slave to the white man." He would threaten to kill me. He almost single-handedly destroyed my self-esteem by talking down to me all the time, calling me names and treating me like I was less than a woman and less than human. No one has ever believed me but my mother and my sisters, because I would call them whenever he would rage and they would hear him on the other end of the phone. I held them close, as I still do to this day. They served as my outlet and my support system.

With his constant outbursts and abuse, my living situation became unbearable. After arguing almost daily, he would resort to physical violence. We went to see a counselor once and this was a good step, but it was a step taken too late, in my opinion. Eventually, I learned that he did not love himself because if he loved himself, he would have loved me, and not treated me this way. Know this — when you do not love yourself, you have the tendency to hurt other people, and you may not realize it actually hurts their emotions, mental health, self-esteem, or otherwise. We must be mindful of how we treat and interact with others, because we never know how this may affect them.

You must see that one's future is important and to be in a healthy environment is a no-brainer. It takes boldness to make decisions that you know are the best for your journey in life. I did not want my children to try to function in a home of dysfunction. I do not believe parents who argue every day is healthy for anyone. I was subject to my partner's abusive physical, mental, and verbal nature constantly. I believe in making the right choices for the well-being of everyone, especially my children. I am a woman who was once a little girl. In my opinion, they should not be in a home environment that is stressful due to daily nonsense disagreements that are clearly a path to poor mental health. This is not fair to them. In situations similar to this, do not second-guess yourself.

In relationships, sometimes one partner will seek to make the other powerless and this does not benefit either person. When any person's unique power is dimmed or diminished, the evolution that could have otherwise occurred, may stagnate the beauty that would have otherwise manifested through the power and uniqueness that both people brought to the relationship. One's essence should not be quenched. It should be allowed to blossom and thrive, all things considered.

I have always been optimistic and filled with joy ever since I was a little girl. I grew up in a place called Eatonton, Georgia, home of Alice Walker and birthplace of the Uncle Remus Museum. I remember running through open fields, playing with my younger sister, and using my creative imagination. This was the joy of life to me. As I grew older, being optimistic despite trying situations was often the only solution. I almost always try to see the silver lining in everything! Even in the situation with my then husband, I tried to remain positive. You know, once someone has the key to your optimism and the joy in your life, it is difficult to get those gems back. Realizing that one's upbringing is a significant part of their existence and life experience may cause you to believe this is normal behavior.

I am determined to be "Lipstick Red." My courage is perhaps what I am most thankful for in life. Not having courage is not an option. Having courage made all the difference in who I am today. Despite the challenges and trials that would come later involving my partner, I still overcame them by allowing the God of Israel to be more present in my life. To remain hopeful and faithful that over my life I have made some good choices and have been blessed because of it has made all of the difference. I grew up with faith in God. I relied on and continue to rely on Him and His Word to guide me. The woman I was before I got married had to be reformed and renewed, and that only came with trusting in God's provision. 2 Corinthians 4:17 (King James Version Holy Bible) says, "For our light affliction, which is but for a moment, worketh for us a far more exceeding and eternal weight of glory." The Bible also says in 2 Timothy 3:11, "Persecutions, afflictions...what persecutions I endured: but out of them all Christ delivered me." He delivered me from something that was on a path of destruction and I chose to be bold and get out. Get out! Despite all my hardships, those experiences allowed me to grow and learn. You are the vessel for your own essence and no one gets to silence and suppress your destiny-not even your partner. Not even you. Be bold!

You do not deserve to be held captive, abused, mistreated, taken advantage of, or disrespected...by anyone. You were not created by God for this mess. If your husband, partner, spouse, friend, etc. does not value you, do not allow it to continue. You are better than this, [insert your name here]. Be brave. Leave and do not return. Be confident that you made the best decision for yourself. It will make all of the difference. This is just one example of being bold. Your version of bold may look different, depending on what is going on in your life. I encourage you to just take a risk. I encourage you to remove yourself from any negative or hurtful situation. You will be just fine. You have to realize your worth as a woman.

Despite my circumstances, I mustered up the strength to be bold and take charge of my life. If you are in a similar situation, be bold enough to know what's good for you and take that leap! You can do it! You can reclaim what is rightfully yours.

Now is an excellent time to repeat the mantra introduced in the introduction:

"I am "Lipstick, Red!" I am bold. I am beautiful. I am daring. I am confident. I am graceful. I am timeless. I am unmatched. I am uniquely me! From the hair on top of my head, to the brain I have inside…from the fullness of my breasts, no matter what size, to my hips that give me my core, and from my gorgeous legs…I

am "Lipstick, Red!" I am me. I am unique and this is my decree."

You must exercise your bold. How do you feel about your ability to take that next step? Are you confident and courageous? Believe in it! Step out and show it! In your daily life choices at home, at work, through shopping, cooking, learning, and everything and anything in between, you must be bold. That is just a small fraction of what you need to express your true femininity. Ignite your bold! To be bold is to be "Lipstick Red."

Here I have created my own definition of boldness. I encourage you to do the same and figure out what it means to you:

My Bold: To accept my "womanness." Don't think twice…make it happen!

Womanness defined: "Everything about a woman that she has yet to discover about her own "Self." When she discovers her "Lipstick Red," she discovers the essence of her "self" as

a true woman. She can now live as she was destined to live and be who she is destined to be."

What is your Bold, [insert your name here]? Think about it and write it down, that way you can go back and refer to it as needed. The 'Reader's Notes' section is the perfect place to jot it down.

Chapter 3: Reader's Notes

Chapter 4 - "Lipstick, Red" is Beautiful

"Beauty begins the moment you decide to be yourself." - Coco Chanel

[Insert your name here], do you really believe you are beautiful? Do you believe in your inner and outward beauty? All of us as women have our own characteristics that make us unique. You may have heard that "beauty is skin deep." This is the measure of our kindness, integrity, and compassion. But both inner *and* outer beauty belong to us; this is a part of our art. Our imperfections and things we wish to hide or wished were different make us who we are. From our curves to our hair to our skin tone, any variation is beautiful. Women, we are *fine*. We are exquisite. [Insert your name here], when was the last time you acknowledged that fact?

Once you believe and accept that you are beautiful and of rare quality, this is an amazing thing. The world looks a bit differently to you from your new perspective. You begin to value and show yourself love. It is so important to be kind to yourself and respect yourself as a person. Don't hide your beauty. Don't deny it. Don't keep it in a box. You are wonderfully made. Forget about those who don't see or acknowledge that. Focus on how *you* see yourself.

My beauty came full circle when I put myself in check one day. When I attended high school, I said, "Arletha, there are so many girls in the world and you are one of them. Everyone has his or her own uniqueness and identity. It is impossible for me to be her and it is impossible for her to be me, because that's just not the way the God of Israel wanted it to be. Be the best 'you.' Your gifts will make room for you. All you have to do is believe."

Your beauty comes when *you* decide that you love yourself enough to be you. Though society has led us to believe beauty is what it dictates, in reality it is not. No one is the same, so how can beauty be what and who it defines as beautiful? Don't change for the world. Exist in your own flesh, in your own skin, in your own self. Don't redefine it. All women must accept themselves and channel the confident and classy "Lipstick Red" woman they were naturally born to be. And that is done by seeing your differences and uniqueness as beautiful.

Say to yourself, "I like myself because I am me...There is no one else I'd rather be" (Karen Beaumont *I Like Myself!*).

How do you captivate your beauty each day? What is it you do to represent beauty in the way only you can do it? Step out of that box, [insert your name here]!

Once again, recite to yourself this message of encouragement:

"I am "Lipstick, Red!" I am bold. I am beautiful. I am daring. I am confident. I am graceful. I am timeless. I am unmatched. I am

uniquely me! From the hair on top of my head, to the brain I have inside…from the fullness of my breasts, no matter what size, to my hips that give me my core, and from my gorgeous legs…I am "Lipstick, Red!" I am me. I am unique and this is my decree."

Here is *my* definition of beautiful. Think about what beauty means to *you* and how you find ways to express that beauty, whether it be inwardly or outwardly:

My Beautiful: Being pleased about everything that is uniquely me and who I am, no matter what. I am beautifully me and you are beautifully you.

What is your beautiful?

Chapter 4: Reader's Notes

Chapter 5 - "Lipstick, Red" is Daring

"Knowing what must be done does away with fear." - Rosa Parks

Are you willing to take risks, [insert your name here]? When you are "Lipstick Red," to be daring is second nature. It just comes so effortlessly. Whether it be through a STEM career, fashion, sex, job decisions, travel, creating something, whatever — are you willing to try something new and spice up your life? Are you daring enough to express yourself? Are you daring enough to try?

Likewise, are you being called to donate a large sum to a charity? Do you feel compelled to speak out about an injustice, or issue you care about? Get out of that box, [insert your name here]! What is holding you back? What is stopping you from being vibrant, expressive, courageous, and daring? More often than not, you are standing in your own way, but this can change. Believe in yourself and be the daring woman you were destined and designed to be.

[Insert your name here], what is the most daring thing(s) you have done in your lifetime? What daring things do you wish to do, but find yourself to be a bit hesitant? What nudge do you need to make them happen? Do you want to launch a business? Do you want to have a career in science, technology, engineering, mathematics, or the arts? Are you in the way of yourself?

Repeat after me:

"I am "Lipstick, Red!" I am bold. I am beautiful. I am daring. I am confident. I am graceful. I am timeless. I am unmatched. I am uniquely me! From the hair on top of my head, to the brain I have inside...from the fullness of my breasts, no matter what size, to my hips that give me my core, and from my gorgeous legs...I

am "Lipstick, Red!" I am me. I am unique and this is my decree."

This is my personal definition of being daring:

My Daring: When I get the desire or urge to do…I do and have no regrets. It has made such a difference in my daily life! To be daring should never be at the expense of someone's physical or mental wellbeing. You must always have dignity and class. No exceptions!

What about you, [insert your name here]? What's your version of daring?

Chapter 5: Reader's Notes

Chapter 6 - "Lipstick, Red" is Confident

"Above all, be the heroine of your life, not the victim." - Nora Ephron

Confidence is the assuredness you have in that you've made the right decisions for yourself. It is a lack of fear and a refusal to continuously question yourself. It is to go forth bravely. When it comes to confidence, it is imperative that you believe in yourself, and then exemplify it through your actions. How do you show confidence?

When you know that you know what you know, this makes the biggest difference. Be confident in your knowledge, intelligence, and talents. Don't let doubt cloud your judgment. Don't let negative thoughts creep up that cause you to waver. Cast away those things that hinder you from believing that you got this and you know your stuff. In the words of the Disney movie, *Frozen*, "Let It Go!" You must move what you have in your "box" to confidence in and with your womanness. Let nothing stagnate your potential for growth.

"Lipstick Red" confidence makes all the difference. You see it in the women you admire. It exudes and radiates this certain magic. The way they carry themselves is how you want to feel. It's infectious. Women, we must realize that we are *all* "Lipstick Red" magical. Embrace who you are every day and it will change your life. Believe in your womanness. Feel comfortable with your womanness. Be the example of womanness. So many young girls and other women are looking up to you. Your womanness is powerful beyond measure. Get to know your expression of "Lipstick Red" confidence, and live it. Wear confidence with class and dignity because it never goes out of style!

It may seem redundant, but repetition often leads to memorization. Remember to always remind yourself of this message, as it gets you in the habit of thinking more positively about yourself:

"I am "Lipstick, Red!" I am bold. I am beautiful. I am daring. I am confident. I am graceful. I am timeless. I am unmatched. I am uniquely me! From the hair on top of my head, to the brain I have inside...from the fullness of my breasts, no matter what size, to my hips that give me my core, and from my gorgeous legs...I am "Lipstick, Red!" I am me. I am unique and this is my decree."

Can you rely on yourself to express "Lipstick Red?" Are you certain about your expression of womanness? I certainly am. Here's what I believe to be true about confidence:

My Confidence: I am me. There is no one on this green Earth I'd rather be. I know the truth and I live by the truth. I believe in myself and all of my unique abilities. I know who I am and I love me for me. I am who I'd rather be. I also know who my Creator is, and my Creator made no mistakes when it came to creating me. Confidence is key. Don't compromise it! Don't give up on it! Don't ever lose it!

How do you define confidence, [insert your name here]? What are some ways you can use it to your advantage?

Chapter 6: Reader's Notes

Chapter 7 - "Lipstick, Red" is Graceful

"Keep your heels, head, and standards high." - Coco Chanel

When you walk with grace, you have this gentleness about you. It is not necessarily to say that you are delicate or fragile, but more so gracious and kind. Do you believe you are graceful [insert your name here]? How do you walk with grace?

The art of a woman is graceful. The way we move, the way we believe, the way we say things, and the way we get stuff done is graceful in its purest form. Make no mistake about it — to possess the gift of grace is just as magical as any other quality. It is something all women have inside and out. On the outside, it's your essence, chic hair style, the way you warmly smile, the way words flow out of your mouth with power and conviction, the way you intentionally work at something with your hands... it's all graceful. Inside, it is merely manifested in the way you treat others — your tender heart. You are an embodiment of grace. You must learn to guard it. If no one ever told you, now you know. You are naturally beautiful. You must guard your grace because it is a very precious and valuable prize to behold.

How can you enhance your grace? In what ways do you try to exemplify the art of gracefulness? It should be important to you because it further defines us as women. Take your gracefulness to another level, [insert your name here]! See and feel the difference it can make in your life. No one has your elegance. No one has your way of conversing with other people. No one else walks like you. No one else *is* you. So tap into that. Discover your gracefulness. It will unlock a door to meaningfulness all around you, and allow you to touch the world in your own special way. When you realize you have it, you will know.

I encourage you to proclaim:

"I am "Lipstick, Red!" I am bold. I am beautiful. I am daring. I am confident. I am graceful. I am timeless. I am unmatched. I am uniquely me! From the hair on top of my head, to the brain I have inside…from the fullness of my breasts, no matter what size, to my hips that give me my core, and from my gorgeous legs…I am "Lipstick, Red!" I am me. I am unique and this is my decree."

Here is what I think being graceful means:

My Graceful: Is bringing all qualities of "Lipstick Red" to the table and being the essence of all of them, fully and without question. My graceful is also to be elegant, stylish, refined, sophisticated, poised, beautiful, polished, natural, confident, and to be me. I am graceful.

What is your 'Graceful,' [insert your name]? I challenge you to recognize the grace you have within you.

Chapter 7: Reader's Notes

Chapter 8 - "Lipstick, Red" is Timeless

"A girl ("Lipstick Red" Woman) should be two things: classy and fabulous." - Coco Chanel

The color red has been and will always be timeless. It will always be striking. It will always be gorgeous. What about you? Will you always be timeless? Will your character stand the test of time?

It is important that at no matter what age, we uphold the concept of "Lipstick Red." If we do not value these qualities throughout life, we will not understand the true meaning of our "womanness" nor what we stand for as women. How do you define yourself? More importantly, what will people remember about you? Yes, "Lipstick Red" is a choice, but it is also necessary in building up positive attributes that are crucial to thrive. Timelessness surrounds all of these essentials. When we are timeless, we possess an upstanding character that far surpasses anything superficial things could give us. We have meaning. The mere fact that we were born as women is something that can never be disregarded. We are women, first.

In an article by Kat Kou entitled, "War, Women, and Lipstick" (http://medium.com/glossary/lipstick-676854e83d5d), the following was noted related to our topic "Lipstick Red": "Lipstick is the most treasured and essential item that women cannot live without, and the shade that has the most culturally staying power is red." There is also a "rich history lavished in identity, freedom and liberation. Red lips have been a signature look in fashion for more than 5,000 years, and it exudes sexuality, mystery, and power. Throughout the centuries, it's been worn by women to feel bolder, stronger, and more confident. Women during the suffrage movement in the early 1900's wore it to defy the norm, and the factory-working woman considered her lipstick as part of her armour as she struggled to make her way through World War II." Finally, but not least, "In 1912, Elizabeth Arden, owner of the Red Door Salon on Fifth Avenue in New York City, participated in the suffrage movement, and supplied her own self-designed lipstick called "Red Door Red" to women going through the turbulent time. With an intention for the color to symbolize hope, power, and strength, the striking shade of lipstick became a symbol of female solidarity, and fearlessness." Therefore, as "Lipstick Red" women, you have the unique opportunity to embrace this banner of confidence knowing that "Lipstick Red" has meaning. You are a woman of hope, power, strength, fearlessness and much, much more. You are bold, beautiful, daring, confident, graceful, timeless and unmatched.

Red lipstick has been around for centuries, it was even with the Egyptians who are known for the rich civilization they had centuries ago. Therefore, it is timeless. When you are a woman who is timeless, you will never go out of style. This starts with seeing yourself for who you are and embracing your art and grace as a "Lipstick Red" woman.

Again, what makes you timeless [insert your name here]? Red lipstick makes a bold statement. See for yourself. It can certainly stand alone. It is my favorite color of lipstick, because it represents dignity, class, elegance, strength, beauty, and so much more. It is my favorite because it can be worn with just about everything you have in your closet. I especially like it because it represents me. It is classic. What move will you make to be timeless? What qualities about yourself can you use to show exemplary character? "Lipstick Red" is unique, and you are too. We are bold, beautiful, daring, confident, graceful, timeless, and unmatched. We have class, elegance, and dignity as women. Red lipstick is memorable and has a lasting impression. Adapt to your timelessness. Say to yourself, "I am 'Lipstick Red!'"

Remind yourself of this familiar truth:

"I am "Lipstick, Red!" I am bold. I am beautiful. I am daring. I am confident. I am graceful. I am timeless. I am unmatched. I am uniquely me! From the hair on top of my head, to the brain I have inside...from the fullness of my breasts, no matter what size, to my hips that give me my core, and from my gorgeous legs...I am "Lipstick, Red!" I am me. I am unique and this is my decree."

Here's how I define my timelessness:

My Timeless: I choose to be "Lipstick Red." I choose to embrace all things that are classy, fabulous, ageless, and lasting. I choose to embrace my uniqueness as a woman. I choose to be bold, beautiful, daring, confident, graceful, timeless, unmatched, classy, and elegant.Will you do the same?

What about you? What is your version of 'Timeless,' [insert your name here]?

Chapter 8: Reader's Notes

Chapter 9 - "Lipstick Red" is Unmatched

"Lipstick Red" is you and it is also me. Like the various shades of red lipstick, you are uniquely you and I am uniquely me." - A. Williams

What is the first thing that comes to mind when you think of the word "unmatched?" It means nothing can rival whatever 'it' is; nothing can compare. To be "Lipstick Red" is to be unmatched. There are many different kinds of women throughout the world, quite like there are different shades of red lipstick. However, each of these colors are still uniquely powerful and wondrous in their own existence as a unique shade of red. The same applies to women. Our own "Lipstick Red" uniqueness is unmatched. Therefore, there is no match for you...right? Likewise, there is no match for me. No one on this planet can do what you do, say what you say, or be how you are as perfectly as you can.

See how other women embrace their own "Lipstick Red." Some are well known and some are not, but what matters most is that they have an understanding about their own unique identity and have come into the fullness of their individual power. What will you do to channel your "Lipstick Red?" What will you do to come into the fullness of yourself?

Think about ways you can take on the "Lipstick Red" persona. Think about ways you can express your own bold, beautiful, daring, confident, graceful, timeless, unmatched, classy, elegant, and dignified self. These attributes are indeed meaningful and you already have them inside you.

The world is waiting for you, [insert your name here]. Express yourself in your own fullness as a woman and see how your expression can make a difference in the world.

"Lipstick Red" is you and it is also me. It is also the woman right next to you. It is the woman in the next room. It is the woman on the next aisle. It is the woman in the office you frequent. It is the woman in the office you've never met. It is the woman you see and it is the women you do not see and it is the woman you ignore.

I am "Lipstick, Red!" I am bold. I am beautiful. I am daring. I am confident. I am graceful. I am timeless. I am unmatched. I am uniquely me! From the hair on top of my head, to the brain I have inside…from the fullness of my breasts, no matter what size, to my hips that give me my core, and from my gorgeous legs…I am "Lipstick, Red!" I am me. I am unique and this is my decree."

"I am "Lipstick, Red!" I am bold. I am beautiful. I am daring. I am confident. I am graceful. I am timeless. I am unmatched. I am uniquely me! From the hair on top of my head, to the brain I have inside…from the fullness of my breasts, no matter what size, to my hips that give me my core, and from my gorgeous legs, all

the way to my feet, which have carried me this far...I am "Lipstick, Red!" I am me. I am unique and this is my decree."

This is how I personally view being unmatched:

My Unmatched: I will not be equally matched with what is common. Lack of "womanness" is not my expectation. Walking in my newly defined and unmatched "Lipstick Red," I shall not settle for less. Your unmatched "womanness" is within you and it is a gift. I have opened mine, what about you ? - What will it take for you to open yours?

What is your Unmatched?

Chapter 9: Reader's Notes

Chapter 10 - "Lipstick, Red" Does Not Envy

"There is a special place in hell for women who do not help other women." - Madeleine Albright

A woman who is "Lipstick Red" does not envy. In fact, she embraces the truth of every woman in her "womanness." She can look at another woman, admire what she has, and respect her without feeling threatened. Envying other women is not an option and is never encouraged. We never know another woman's story. We may never know her truth. We never know the paths in her life that brought her to where she is today. Do not judge. Do not envy. She is "Lipstick Red" too. When you come across a person who makes you feel off balance, it's okay to avoid them. Sometimes, our discerning spirit nudges us and lets us know where to go and where not to go, i.e., who to approach and who not to approach. You are encouraged to follow that voice. If someone feels toxic, detrimental to your journey, or yes, even makes you feel insecure, it is okay to disassociate for your own sanity. However, if there is an opportunity, encourage other women in their strengths or success.

Envious women stagnate their own growth and while you are worried and jealous about someone else's goodness, grace, and blessings, you will not flourish. Embrace other women for their success and accomplishments. Leave alone what is not meant for you and focus on what is. When you come into the fullness of your essence, you should be directing your attention to your needs and your purpose.

[Insert your name here], you must seek to live your days such that the "Lipstick Red" principles are at the forefront. Again, when we envy other women who are in touch with their womanness, it can cause conflict in our own atmosphere and reflect negatively on you and what you are trying to accomplish. Instead, we must simply be happy for other women and uplift them.You can then use their success as inspiration in order to motivate you. Show up! Get into your essence. Make a "Lipstick Red" difference in our world. Shine!

It's imperative to know that you can't have another person's "womanness," because you were given your own. Strive to perfect and polish your own journey so that you can walk with the same boldness, beauty, daring, confidence, grace, timelessness, and unmatched "womanness" you see around you. Remember, "Lipstick Red" does not envy...it has dignity. Always have dignity and don't ever compromise it.

As you know, there is a proclamation that says:

"I am "Lipstick, Red!" I am bold. I am beautiful. I am daring. I am confident. I am graceful. I am timeless. I am unmatched. I am

uniquely me! From the hair on top of my head, to the brain I have inside...from the fullness of my breasts, no matter what size, to my hips that give me my core, and from my gorgeous legs...I am "Lipstick, Red!" I am me. I am unique and this is my decree."

There is a "Lipstick Red" Golden Rule: Thou Shall Not Envy Other Women. It will hinder your essence as a woman. To envy is to fail all that we seek to gain. To envy is to set ourselves up to fail in and with all we seek to gain.

Remember, come into the center of your CORE (Center of Renewed Essence). You will not let yourself down because you have a center of focus and are working toward your full "womanness." It is a beautiful thing to know. It is a beautiful thing to possess...go ahead and tap into it!

Chapter 10: Reader's Notes

Chapter II - The Essence of "The Woman"

"Do you want to meet the love of your life? Look in the mirror." - Byron Katie

Why does it seem like a woman's art and grace has been diluted? If you aren't sure, let me clue you in on something. Our essence has been undervalued and guess what? We can do something about it. Women are often not held in high regard, but we can change that by valuing ourselves and encouraging the women around us. It's time we support each other. Can we please hit the red RESET button on this issue?

Essence is *"the most significant element, quality, or aspect of a thing or person,"* and *our* essence is our "womanness;" our art and grace.

Women are a beautiful work of art. We captivate a room with not just our beauty or charm, but our kindness, intelligence, and confidence. We women are powerful. We literally give life to others through biological processes only we have the strength to endure. We have so much to offer -- and it's not just childbearing or being a housewife. We can move mountains and influence nations with our words and our actions.

We cannot allow other people's perception of us to dictate how we live or make us question our worth. We are valuable gems. We are to be cherished and appreciated. But that comes with loving ourselves first. We need to recognize our individual importance, while also realizing our collective worth as women.

The seven attributes that embody "Lipstick Red" are qualities that bring a woman's sparkle, shine, and vibrance to life. They are life-changing characteristics that are certain to boost your self-confidence and make you more aware of the greatness in yourself. The attributes in this book should reveal to you the magic you have been blessed with naturally. All you have to do is take a look at each one of them, and give yourself a positive affirmation with each one by proclaiming:

"I am "Lipstick, Red!" I am bold. I am beautiful. I am daring. I am confident. I am graceful. I am timeless. I am unmatched. I am uniquely me! From the hair on top of my head, to the brain I have inside…from the fullness of my breasts, no matter what size, to my hips that give me my core, and from my gorgeous legs…I am "Lipstick, Red!" I am me. I am unique and this is my decree."

    In conclusion, as a woman, you must live your life each day representing "Lipstick Red" endlessly. The seven attributes we discussed, along with class, dignity, and elegance, are wonderful qualities to possess. Own them! Embrace them! Enjoy them!

Embody them! The only thing stopping you is your unwillingness to believe they will be the difference in who you are now, at this moment, and the woman you are destined to be for eternity after you implement them. Remember, no one is perfect, but that doesn't mean we shouldn't strive to be our very best each and every day.

As a "Lipstick Red" woman, you should now see that your existence is essential; you are a woman of dignity and character. You are encouraged to uphold these qualities for the rest of your life. Teach them to other women, teens, and young girls who need guidance and direction. Like you, they will benefit in their self-esteem.

Lastly, I have found that when I say "Lipstick Red" to myself in silence or aloud, it has been the one thing that reminds me to love myself and keep doing me. The attributes I discuss serve to remind myself of my profound "womanness." I am "Lipstick Red!" Are you? I know you have it in you. Own your "Lipstick Red!" Embrace it! Enjoy it! Embody it! Know that your essence is meaningful. Your essence makes you more aware and in tune with your magic and power. [Insert your name here], own your version of "Lipstick Red." The world needs the particular light only you can give.

Womanness defined: Everything about a woman that she has yet to discover about her own "Self." When she discovers her "Lipstick Red," she discovers the essence of her "self" as a true women. She can now live as she was destined to live and be who she is destined to be."

Chapter II: Reader's Notes

"Lipstick, Red!" Inspirations

"You Are Enough"

A Poem By: Arletha

Inspired by Meghan Markle, Duchess of Sussex

You are enough to make a real difference
You are enough to make a positive change

Whatever you choose to do in life really does matter
Because none of us are the same

No matter where you lived, what you did helped to shape you in some way
Know that we all have a brain to think and be someone other than "gone astray"

We all have gifts and talents the world is yet to know
For it has always been the light inside of us that has been eager to gleam and glow

The world is your stage, even like it's mine
For the seeds you have within will grow, it just takes a little water and sunshine

You may choose philanthropy, advocacy, leadership or just about whatever you'd like
Remember, the world is a precious gift to mankind from God
and we must always strive to do what's right

You are enough to make a real difference
You are enough to make a positive change

When you fulfill the desires of your heart inside,
It is sure to help to magnify your range

You are enough to make a real difference
You are enough to make a positive change

When you dream big and go for what you see,
the world will be the place it should be
Since it was truly a gift from God for both you and me.

"Lipstick Red"
A Poem By: Arletha

1-2-3, I am unique. I am "Lipstick Red!"
Bold, Beautiful, Daring, Confident, Graceful, Timeless, Unmatched…Uniquely Me.
Uniquely me is all I will ever want to be.
Doing it with style, grace, elegance, and class,
Yes, yes, I do have the treasure of uncompromised sass.

No matter what he said, she said…I am "Lipstick Red!"
1-2-3, I am unique. I am "Lipstick Red!"
In the end, it is my womanness that is all that jazz…
It is my uniqueness…my style, grace, elegance, and class.
That ultimately, and most definitely will unveil a glimpse of my confident pizzazz!

The banner for life after a journey filled with questions, lessons, and doubts,
I certainly have what it takes to be the "Lipstick Red" that will make me scream and shout!

1-2-3, I am unique. I am "Lipstick Red."
After a road like this, I have found exactly what I need, nuff said!
Bold, Beautiful, Daring, Confident, Graceful, Timeless, Unmatched...
I am "Lipstick Red!"

"¡Pintalabios rojo!" ¡Yo soy yo!
(Spanish)

"Помада красная!" Я - это я!"
(Russian)

"!أحمر الشفاه أحمر!" أنا أنا
(Arabic)

«Շրթներկ կարմիր»: Ես եմ:
Armenian

"Червило червено!" Аз съм себе си!
(Bulgarian)

"နှုတ်ခမ်းနီနီနီ" ငါပင်ဖြစ်၏။
(Burmese)

"唇膏紅色！"我是我！"
(Chinese)

"Crveni ruž!" Ja sam ja!"
(Croatian)

"Lipstick Red!" Ako ay ako!"
(Filipino)

"Rouge à lèvres rouge!" Je suis moi!"
(French)

"Lippenstift rot!" Ich bin ich!"
(German)

"Lipstick Red!" Owau no Me! "
(Hawaiian)

"Leppestift rød!" Jeg er meg!"
(Norwegian)

"립스틱 레드!" 나는 나니까!"
(Korean)

「リップスティックレッド！」私は私です！"
(Japanese)

"Rossetto rosso!" Io sono me!"
(Italian)

"שפתון אדום!" אני אני!"
(Hebrew)

Batom vermelho!" Eu sou eu!"
(Portuguese)

"Šminka rdeča!" Jaz sem jaz! "
Slovenian)

"Lipstick Nyekundu!" Mimi ndiye! "
(Swahili)

"Läppstift röd!" Jag är jag!"
(Swedish)

"Lipstick Red" Reflections

*My "Lipstick Red" Journal
(20 Questions/Reflections)*

What does "Lipstick Red" mean to you?

In what ways are you a "Lipstick Red" woman?

What is one of your favorite quotes in the book?

What was pivotal for you as you read through "Lipstick Red! I Am Me!"?

_____
_____
_____
_____
_____
_____
_____
_____
_____
_____
_____
_____

In what ways will you now unleash your bold, beautiful, daring, confident, graceful, timeless and unmatched "Self?"

_____
_____
_____
_____
_____
_____
_____
_____
_____
_____
_____

If you could share "Lipstick Red! I Am Me" with other women and girls, who would you share it with?

Do you know the gift(s) you are meant to share with the world? If so, what are they?

What do you dream about for yourself?

_____

_____

_____

_____

_____

_____

_____

_____

_____

_____

_____

_____

In what ways will you OR are you a sphere of influence for other women, girls, and humanity?

_____

_____

_____

_____

_____

_____

_____

_____

_____

_____

_____

In what ways are you improving yourself?

How are you finding joy in each day?

In what ways are you planning to become the woman you were destined to be?

What do you absolutely love about who you are in this moment?

In what ways are you listening to the desires of your "Self?"

_____

_____

_____

_____

_____

_____

_____

_____

_____

_____

_____

_____

How can you freely embrace yourself as a
"Lipstick Red" woman?

Which "Lipstick Red" attribute(s) did you identify with the most? Why?

Will you challenge yourself to jot down your "Lipstick Red" moments and how it influenced your decision(s)?

_____

_____

_____

_____

_____

_____

_____

_____

_____

_____

_____

What is it about your uniqueness you wish others would understand?

Over the next years if your life, in what ways do you plan to embody "Lipstick Red! I Am Me"?

While you are on your "Lipstick Red" journey, will you promise yourself that you will not find any substitute for the essence of your womanness? Why is this important to you?

_____
_____
_____
_____
_____
_____
_____
_____
_____
_____
_____
_____

www.ingramcontent.com/pod-product-compliance
Lightning Source LLC
Chambersburg PA
CBHW030155100526
44592CB00009B/290